SIMPLE ETIQUETTE IN

ILLUSTRATED BY
IRENE SANDERSON

SIMPLE ETIQUETTE IN

Helmut Morsbach

WITH A FOREWORD BY
RONALD DORE

Simple Books Limited
Sandgate, Folkestone, Kent

SIMPLE ETIQUETTE IN JAPAN

Simple Books Ltd
Knoll House, 35 The Crescent, Sandgate,
Folkestone, Kent, England.

First published 1984
© Helmut Morsbach

ISBN 0-904404-46-3

Reprinted 1986
Reprinted 1990

Distributed in the USA & Canada by:
The Talman Co., Inc.
150 Fifth Avenue
New York, NY 10011

Printed in England by BPCC Wheatons Ltd, Exeter

CONTENTS

FOREWORD

Learning to do as the Tokyoites do is important when you are in Japan. Or rather, at least *trying* to do as the Tokyoites do—for the crucial thing is to demonstrate, by doing so, that one dissociates oneself from the unfortunate past and really does look forward to building relations with one's Japanese opposite numbers on the footing of mutuality, of equality of respect and consideration.

So the trying is the important thing, at least for building up *rapport*. It is a perfectly viable strategy to profess a combination of total ignorance of Japanese manners and a total willingness to be instructed. And sometimes it can even be the best strategy. Those who are trying to conform to conventions that have not become second nature can sometimes become anxious about doing the right thing, and that can introduce a tension into the relationship which actually militates against *rapport*.

Don't worry, therefore, if, when you are in mid-situation, you forget one of the wise injunctions to be found in Dr Morsbach's book. Just break off to ask your Japanese friends what is the right thing to do and they will not think the worse of you for it, because although *they* feel obliged to show familiarity with western customs, they don't really *expect* foreigners to know theirs—because of all the history of the last hundred years.

But if you can manage *not* to forget Helmut Morsbach's good advice, so much the better. He has spent a long time asking people what should properly be done in all kinds of situations, and gives an excellent summary of what one might call the etiquette of consciousness.

But he also gives more than that. As a shrewd observer of the behaviour of Japanese and other peoples he has noticed some of the characteristically Japanese ways of behaving which the Japanese will *not* tell you about because they tend to take them for granted, to think of them as part of human nature and not particularly a matter of 'doing as the Tokyoites do'. His special interest is in all those ways people have of communicating without words.

Since visitors to Japan who are not going to spend years learning the Japanese language before they go may find verbal communication restricted on occasion, Helmut Morsbach's shrewd observations on gesture language should be particularly useful.

Even someone like me who has been an occasional visitor to Japan for the last 30 years can profit from Dr Morsbach's book—partly from enjoying the accuracy of his observations, but not least from the reassurance that comes from discovering that one has been getting some things wrong for 30 years, but in spite of that can still keep one's Japanese friends!

Ronald Dore

INTRODUCTION

In Japan, traditional etiquette continues to be extremely important, despite whatever outward appearances of 'westernisation' the visitor may experience.

When arriving on business, for example, you will automatically be accorded a relatively high status, and experience polite treatment by those who matter.

Most Japanese expect that as a foreigner you will behave according to western rules and conditioning. However, they can always be forgiven for hoping that at some point you will at least try to understand their ways.

This book, therefore, is an attempt to highlight some of the key facets of Japanese mores and customs that can at least be committed to memory and grasped intellectually before letting experience and instinct take their course.

Although addressed principally to the visiting businessman, *Simple Etiquette in Japan* will I hope help 'prepare the ground' for all those who have the opportunity to discover this remarkable culture and its people.

H.M.

ACKNOWLEDGEMENTS:
Several friends have read the original draft and made useful suggestions, especially my publisher, Paul Norbury, as well as Professors Ronald Dore and Yoko Sano.
Naturally I have profited from reading many books on Japan, most of all from the thorough (but sometimes outdated) *Japanese Etiquette—an Introduction,* published in 1955 by the Tokyo YWCA.

1

IN GENERAL

Japanese etiquette emphasises courteous behaviour among members belonging to a certain group. If you are properly introduced to such a group, courtesies will be shown to you as well. How should you behave, since the degree of courtesy is generally much higher than in your own culture?

Naturally, it is not expected that you know all about (or even use) the intricate Japanese ways of behaviour, and you would certainly be considered strange if you did. Instead, try to be more polite than at home, since you will be making many *faux pas* whatever you do.

Effusive thanks for minor matters are common in Japan. Therefore try to express your own gratitude more often than at home. For instance, remember to say, 'Thank you for your kindness the other day' on meeting again (see p. 33 for translation), even if this 'kindness' was so general that you would not normally have bothered referring to it.

Japanese still prefer bowing to each other on being introduced. To you, however, they will offer their hand, and will probably attempt a combination of handshake and slight bow. Don't grip the hand too tightly, and don't expect a 'strong' handshake in return. If no hand is offered, imitate the bow you receive as regards depth and frequency. Keep your arms straight and let the palms slide down your thighs while lowering your torso.

On greeting, or during conversation, don't insist on too much eye contact—this tends to be avoided and may be regarded as impolite. Downward glances and limp handshakes should not be interpreted as 'shiftiness' or a sign of a 'weak character'.

Smiling may be a way of hiding embarrassment. Don't take it to mean assent all the time. Most Japanese turn up the corners of their mouth when speaking their own language, and thus seem to be engaged in happy banter more than they really are. Genuine happiness is indicated more accurately by creases in the corners of the eye.

Don't point to persons or objects with your index finger—this is rude. Draw attention by using the whole hand, palm turned upwards, in a flowing (not pointing) movement.

Don't express affection in public, except to small children. Avoid slapping backs or holding others by the arm while talking, except perhaps during convivial all-male drinking sessions.

Japanese generally keep a greater distance from each other when talking. Although you might feel uncomfortable and remote, don't move too close.

Loud sniffing during a cold is not regarded as bad manners, but blowing your nose in front of others is.

Some western gestures are unknown in Japan and may be misunderstood. e.g. winking, or shrugging your shoulders.

Become sensitive to vague, indirect cues asking you to do something, e.g. to get you to leave, someone might remark, 'The car is waiting.'

Most Japanese treat money like westerners treat sex—discreetly, even 'shamefully'. There are times in a business context when for services rendered you might be handed money in an envelope and be asked to sign a receipt. To open the envelope indicates lack of trust. If it does contain less money than stated, it might be due to tax having been deducted at source. The change given in stores is usually presented on a plastic dish. It need not be counted to see if it is correct, since to be short-changed is rare. In Japan, despite occasional bribery scandals in government and big business there is a great deal of honesty in everyday transactions.

Haggling over prices is usually not done, either, although a degree of 'negotiating' especially in duty-free shops, is not unknown. If you want to make money gifts special money gift envelopes can be obtained from stationery shops. Banknotes used as gifts should be uncreased (ideally mint) and can be obtained at special counters in banks.

You are not required to tip anybody! In fact, to attempt to do so could be regarded as insulting.

Exclamations of *Hai, hai* do not signal agreement (as your dictionary tells you); rather, they indicate that the person you are talking to is still listening. Therefore try to exchange something in writing concerning any decisions, such as exact time and location of a meeting.

In a culture where males precede females, you may embarrass a lady if you open a door for her, or offer her your seat. This may imply that she is physically weak. Getting in and out of narrow doors (e.g. lifts) can be a problem if both hold back. Some hilarious collisions have occurred this way!

Western businesswomen on their own in Japan might find it easiest to act as they would in the West as regards precedence etc., but not to feel offended on those occasions when this is not accorded to them.

Toilet facilities for males and females are sometimes unsegregated. A poker face at the urinal helps when ladies suddenly walk past behind you.

While being cocooned by the attentiveness of your hosts and the hotel staff looking after you in Japan, you may at times also witness scenes at odds with 'polite behaviour'. Commuters on trains and buses face this daily during rush hour. Pushing and overcrowding are endured silently. Dozing off while being wedged in somewhere is one way to cope. Once away from the in-group, behaviour can change drastically.

With its complex and colourful history and culture Japan is a fascinating topic to read about. It is well worth the trouble reading as widely as you can before leaving. In Japan, all the major hotels stock considerable quantities of English-language books and journals. Japanese bookshops with special departments for western books on Japan are Maruzen (central Tokyo and Kyoto), and Kinokuniya (Shinjuku and Shibuya areas of Tokyo as well as the Hankyū Railway Station of Osaka).

2
BUSINESS MATTERS

Introductions to a new business contact important to you, should ideally be made by a respected and trustworthy go-between who knows both parties.

Dress well, but conservatively, avoiding flashy colours. The Japanese for 'suit' is 'sebiro', which comes from the name 'Savile Row', London. Allied with this is good deportment; too relaxed a bearing can be interpreted as sign of a 'crooked spirit'.

To further harmony, Japanese conversation mostly allows the partners to agree. Contentious issues are avoided. Refusals, if necessary, tend to be more indirect. 'No' (*'iie'*) sounds harsh and is rarely used. Instead get used to (and use) 'well, maybe', or 'do you think so', or apply the art of pausing. (It could be said, of course, that since the Japanese are more conversant than ever before with western character traits, they increasingly expect more direct 'western-style' response in business dealings. But remember, this may only be an intellectual accommodation of western behaviour.)

Since the Japanese value group solidarity, be prepared to be met on arrival and seen off at departure. This holds for important Japanese visitors as well. However, instead of a rendezvous at far-off Narita Airport (56 kms. from central Tokyo) you might suggest the Tokyo City Air Terminal (TCAT), about 2.5 kilometres from Tokyo Station, which has direct bus connections and check-in facilities.

When ushered into a room, sit at the place allocated by your host, since the seat of honour and other positions in decreasing order of importance are usually predetermined, especially in the traditional Japanese house.

Separated from their reference group, Japanese tend to telephone or write back to base frequently, even if there is little news. This is seen as necessary to continue smooth relations. There is no harm in copying this custom with your Japanese group, especially after you return home. Cards at Christmas and New Year are good reminders that you still care.

When introduced, Japanese businessmen will first exchange visiting cards. It pays to have your own right at the start of your visit, ideally with a translation in Japanese on the reverse. Check with your airline about this service well before departure. (There could be a 3—4 week delay in obtaining them.) Cards can often be picked up on arrival in Japan. If you are unable to arrange for cards to be printed, buy blank cards and use your rubber stamp or stick-on address labels as a temporary substitute.

After shaking hands or bowing, hand over your visiting card with a slight bow, receiving one in return from your new acquaintance who may hiss through his teeth while studying your card. This shows that you are an important person. Take your time to study the card received, and ask for a translation of it if it is in Japanese only. Once seated, you can keep it in view on the table or on the arm-rest of your chair. Finally, take the trouble to pocket it with some indication that it is of value to you. Special albums are available to keep such cards sorted for later reference.

Taxi drivers sometimes have trouble finding an address. When lost, they often enquire at a police box *en route*, but this is time-consuming. You can help by requesting written instructions in Japanese or a sketch from your host beforehand. Otherwise ask at your hotel's front desk (called *furonto*) for written instructions.

Japanese generally prefer discussing business in the hotel's reception area and not in your bedroom. If unacceptable, suggest moving to a coffee shop or a bar.

Since Japanese wives are mostly excluded when their husbands entertain on business, western wives are rarely invited either. However, western wives are increasingly invited to more informal functions.

3

WINING & DINING

In Japan you will be offered Japanese tea at all hours as a matter of course. It is served hot without sugar or milk, in a teacup without a handle. This slightly bitter, green tea, refreshing once you are used to it, can be slurped (but don't overdo this).

If you venture out alone you may be refused entry into certain Japanese food/drink establishments. Most are like English clubs where newcomers (Japanese included) are required to be 'introduced' by regulars. Furthermore, the Japanese fear that you probably don't know enough about local customs to cope on your own. Don't be offended—this is rarely an anti-foreigner bias as such. Try instead to go with a Japanese friend or acquaintance and all will be well.

On being invited out to a Japanese meal and asked about your food preferences, it is usually best to say that anything will be all right, since it is the host's task to order. Such vagueness is not a sign that you are indiscriminate or indifferent: Japanese typically go along with their host's choice as well, preferring not to be different. If there are items in the selection that you then don't like, just leave them untouched and concentrate on the rest.

Before starting you may be handed a small folded towel (*oshibori*), which is steamed hot in winter and is offered either hot or cold in summer. (You may well have been introduced to this splendid custom on your flight to Japan.) Take the towel from its sleeve and unfold it. Men can wipe their face with it, then their arms and hands. Women usually wipe their hands only. Later, during the meal, the *oshibori* can be re-folded and used to wipe your fingers.

Ideally, the meal starts when everyone bows slightly and says, *itadakimas'* ('I will receive')—rather like *bon appetit* in French.

If the meal is traditional Japanese food you can try and overcome your ignorance of conventional eating habits by taking the obvious course of imitating someone sitting close to you. If you are the guest of honour, you might have to start first, but after that it may be best simply to 'follow my leader'.

Many Japanese dishes are served with the primary purpose of looking beautiful. But there are others, such as *tempura* (deep fried fish and vegetables) which are nutritious and appeal to westerners probably because of their western (Portuguese) origin. Even so, care will be taken to harmonise food shapes and colours with matching receptacles.

To the uninitiated western palate, a lot of Japanese food tastes rather bland. For Japanese it is not only the tastiness which is important, but also the food's consistency when felt with one's tongue inside the mouth (e.g. rice grains, slices of raw fish). Suspend your judgement at first (as with many things in Japan), and persevere. You might grow to enjoy judging food by criteria different from your own.

A proper Japanese meal always includes rice. Other dishes are added, depending on how elaborate the meal is. Instead of a succession of courses, most Japanese food is served all at once. The guest is then required to take small portions from each dish without neglecting any. Don't linger too long over one kind of food. Naturally, as a foreigner you can leave untouched any dish you don't like.

Before starting, remove the rice bowl lid and place it upside down on the left. Then put the soup bowl cover similarly on the right.

Japanese prefer brand-new chopsticks (*hashi*) which are made of wood and split apart before use. Scrape one against the other to check for the absence of splinters. Pick the chopsticks up with your right hand and begin by eating the rice.

Chopsticks are really not that difficult to master, provided you put in some practice. Firstly, wedge the lower chopstick firmly in the crotch of your hand, holding it in place by the base of the thumb and the tip of the ring finger. It must not move! Then hold the upper chopstick quite independently, like a pen, between the tips of thumb, index finger and middle finger. Practice holding them one at a time. Then align both tips by pushing them against a flat surface. Try picking up objects by moving the upper tip onto the stationary lower one. Once adept at this, remember not to cross them on putting them down; neither stick them into the rice as a repository.

You can lift the bowls containing rice (as well as soup) to your mouth with your left hand, for the purpose of eating the rice more efficiently.

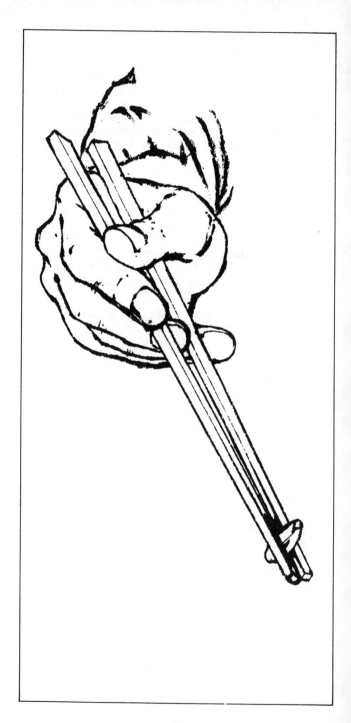

If your rice bowl is empty, ask to have it filled from the large pot. As on all other occasions when giving or receiving something, it is polite to use both hands when lifting the bowl.

Rice left in your bowl indicates that you want more. To show that you have finished, pick out all the grains and eat them.

For dishes from which all guests can help themselves, use the special chopsticks or spoons provided. If absent, reverse your own chopsticks and transfer the food with the clean ends.

Replace the covers of the bowls, and place the chopsticks side-by-side onto the rice bowls or on the special ceramic chopstick rest provided.

Finally, say *gochisō-sama-desh'ta* ('It was a feast', or 'Many thanks for the meal') on leaving, and bow slightly.

Whenever alcohol is served, raise your glass or cup to have it filled, and take a sip before putting it down. Offer to serve others of your party if they have served you: ideally one never pours one's own drinks.

As a sign of esteem or friendship you may be offered another guest's *saké* cup. Accept it with thanks, and raise it to be filled. Later (not immediately) you can offer your cup after having cleaned it, and pour *saké* in return.

The Japanese for 'your health' is *kampai* (lit.: 'a toast'). Incidentally, beer is increasingly drunk instead of *saké* at a Japanese meal. Your empty cup or glass signals to your host that you would like it filled; leave the glass or cup full, therefore, if you don't want any more to drink.

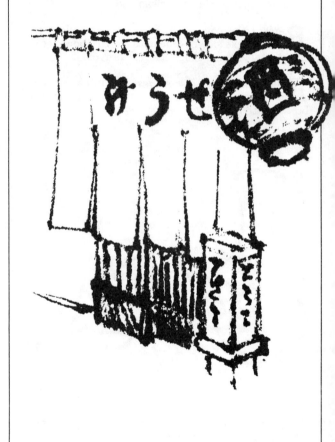

If invited to a bar or night club, enjoy the relaxed atmosphere. Refrain from talking shop and be prepared to sing a few songs when the microphone is passed your way. Some party tricks come in handy here, or the showing of photographs from back home. Don't attempt to pay or offer to 'go Dutch'. However, reciprocate later with some gift, or a counter-invitation to a western restaurant.

If there are hostesses, the one whose English is best will probably be assigned to you, but don't expect this flirtatious atmosphere to lead to anything more. Further insights into the intricacies and etiquette of Japanese night life are best obtained from 'old hands' and other learned sources!

4

THE JAPANESE HOME

As a businessman it will be a rare event to enter your host's home. Some major reasons for this are the following:

● The average Japanese home is much smaller than those in the West and is rarely opened to non-kin.

● Entertaining, even of kin, usually takes place outside the home, in one of the many restaurants, coffee shops, or bars.

● The housewife is usually concerned that her conversational English is poor or non-existent.

● There is the further worry that the foreigner is probably unfamiliar with Japanese customs, e.g. sitting on *tatami* mats, using the squat-type toilet, etc.

● The house may be far from the town, so that the visitor could have problems returning to his/her hotel in the evening.

However, if you *do* get invited, try to remember the following:

On entering the house, remove your shoes in the hallway (*genkan*) before stepping up to the floor of the

house proper. Slippers will be provided, although they are often quite small. Before entering any room laid out with rectangular mats, called *tatami*, leave the slippers behind and proceed in stockinged feet. Treat the *tatami* floor as if it were one large mattress—in such case it makes sense to remove one's footwear!

On or before entering the toilet, look out for the special toilet slippers (often marked 'W.C.') and change into these. Don't forget to change back on leaving the toilet! Since you must always backtrack to recover slippers and shoes, Japanese houses make you feel tied to an invisible rubber band anchored at the *genkan*.

Squatting on one's legs can be painful, even for today's young Japanese used to chairs. You can therefore sit cross-legged (if male), but females (except in jeans) should fold their legs under their bodies, then move the weight off to one side. In some traditional-style rooms there is a recess in the floor (which contains a heater in winter) that is deep enough for your legs. There you can sit almost as if on a chair, especially if a legless back-rest is provided.

One has to squat over the Japanese-style toilet—uncomfortable, but hygienic. The water container above it allows you to wash your hands under the faucet which curves over the bowl-shaped lid. The lever hanging down can be pushed left or right, so that either all the water is released, or just a small amount—a convenient way to save water.

Sometimes the toilet door cannot be locked. Japanese determine whether a toilet is engaged by knocking gently on the outside door, and then wait for a counter-knock to emanate. Unknowing westerners, once inside, sometimes use their body weight in desperation to stop others from entering. The latter, in turn, might think that the door is stuck, and push all the more . . . This 'counter-knocking' custom naturally assumes that the distance between toilet and door is a short one!

To fully appreciate the qualities of a Japanese-style bath you need to take your time and combine cleanliness with relaxation. The bath (*ofuro*) is therefore never in the same room as the toilet.

Undress in the antechamber and place your clothes in one of the baskets provided. Pick up a small towel and enter the bathroom. If others are present, use the towel to hide your nakedness a little. Get a washing bowl and soap, and squat down on a low stool. Scoop some hot water from the tub. Soap your body and rub it, using the towel. Ladle hot water over yourself from the tub, taking care not to get any soap into it.

Since others will use the tub after you, enter it only if you are quite clean. As guest of honour you may be first to use the bath, which could at that stage feel exceedingly hot—much hotter than what you are used to. By all means add some cold water if you don't fancy becoming a boiled lobster.

Of course you need not enter the tub at all, but if you do want to try it, cool part of your anatomy by putting the cold, dripping towel on top of your head. Submerge up to the neck as quickly as possible and then sit quite still—after a few agonising seconds the pain will subside somewhat. Totally immobile, you might even start enjoying this foetal state! Once adapted, stay inside as long as you like, or alternate this with further washing outside.

After leaving the tub, wring the towel and dry yourself—this works surprisingly well. If provided, put on the cotton gown (*yukata*) over your underwear. Take care to wrap the left side over the right, which is customary for both sexes. The reverse is used only once—ie., when you are laid out for the wake, before cremation! Worn with a sash (*obi*), the yukata (provided in all hotels) now serves as a dressing-gown and/or night-gown.

5
GIFT GIVING

Japanese gift-giving is a highly ritualised custom, used mainly as a 'social lubricant' to smooth social interaction. Fortunately, foreigners need not participate fully, but their gifts will be appreciated, leading to return gifts. Three major rules are thus worth remembering:

● *Gifts are always wrapped.* For your unwrapped gifts, get a Japanese friend's help with gift paper and special string. Or buy some gifts in a Japanese shop and ask for your 'naked' gifts to be wrapped as well. You can get fancy paper and ribbons at stationery-shops (*bunbōguya*).

● *A gift, once offered, cannot be refused,* except if it 'smells' like a bribe, in which case it should be returned as soon as possible. Japanese usually belittle their (wrapped) gifts when presenting them. The 'unworthy' receiver should in return express reluctance and initially hesitate to accept. However, this ritualised exchange has only one outcome which is never in doubt. As a foreigner you need not belittle your gift, but don't praise it, either.

● *Japanese traditionally don't open the gift in the presence of the giver*. This allows face to be saved if the gift is much more (or less) expensive than announced. However, if urged to open your gift, you can do so.

Take care not to give too valuable a gift, since equally expensive return presents are usually required of the receiver. This can continue indefinitely, making it very burdensome (and expensive). A gift's major function is not, 'I have plenty, so let's share . . .', or, 'This is for you as a unique individual'. Rather, gifts serve as a balancing of obligations and a continued reminder of the importance of the relationship. Japanese are more finicky here than we are. Get an insider's view if in doubt what to give initially, and what to return.

On receiving a gift, some Japanese might give you a *token return gift* of low value. It is a kind of 'receipt' for your gift—the real return gift will come later. Material gifts can also be given for non-material favours. Get advice whether they are regarded as 'balancing'.

Before departure, buy a number of gifts in your home town, ranging from expensive to inexpensive. Small mementos (even picture post cards of your town) are appreciated as tokens for kindness shown. At the top of the list whisky is a good gift, though bulky and heavy. Buy *boxed* bottles and take the maximum allowed (currently 3). Preferred brands are 'Johnny Walker Black Label' and 'Chivas Regal'; malt whisky is also appreciated.

Luxury foods (from the UK—quality marmalade or tea for example) also make good gifts. (You can re-stock at most Japanese department stores, though at substantially higher prices.) Fortnum and Mason's tea is especially welcomed since this is *not* sold in Japan. Other small gifts can include ties, commemorative coins, photo books and toy models for your host's children.

Most Japanese are keen photographers and will want to take photographs of their friends in a group. Colour prints are subsequently given as small gifts to those in the picture as a matter of courtesy. When you photograph acquaintances and friends in turn, it is a good idea to present them with copies.

Don't admire some art object excessively in your host's house—he might then feel that he should present it to you'!

6

CONVERSATION & COMMUNICATION

Japanese tend not to come to the point straight away, which you might find very tedious at first. After formal introductions, green tea will normally be served. This is a good time for small talk when contentious topics should be avoided. The main topic may be broached much later, or perhaps not at all during the first meeting. Have patience!

Don't be dogmatic in your statements—it is rude to be too direct. Get used to vague and indirect replies, and sense if an atmosphere of mutual trust is developing. If not, try to postpone the discussion of serious matters instead of forcing the issue.

During formal business meetings lengthy monologues—often by the senior person present—are common. If you speak, try to make more pauses than usual so that your Japanese partners can contribute if they want to. Even interpreters, when present, may have trouble understanding you fully without showing it, so check frequently if your point has come across, but without making them look foolish.

Don't use first names for addressing your Japanese partners; rather use 'Mr/Mrs/Miss/Dr X' instead. Alternatively, use their family name, plus -san for everyone except academics, who can be addressed as *sensei* ('teacher'). If you were already on first-name terms with somebody before arrival in Japan, you could discuss whether to continue this, but it is safer to use family name and -san in the presence of others.

Don't be alarmed if you are addressed by your *first* name and -san. Some believe they can be less formal with foreigners (and you could reciprocate). Alternatively, it may be assumed to be your family name, since in Japan family name precedes given name. If you have an unusual given name, avoid confusion by printing it in initials only before your family name on your visiting cards.

Tone down expressions of displeasure, keep a calm face and don't raise your voice. Even then you will probably still appear to be more volatile than most Japanese.

On being introduced to non-English speakers it will sound better if you say something complimentary in your own language than if you utter nothing at all. It is the friendly *intonation* which counts, together with your smile and slight bow.

Photos of your family and home town in a pocket-size album make a good conversation piece, especially if you have language problems. A small dictionary and blank paper are handy to have interesting objects explained to you. Furthermore, you can ask to be taught paper folding (*origami*). In Japan, many activities we consider child-like (or even 'childish') are quite respectable, especially while alcohol is being consumed. On the other hand, a grown-up licking a large ice-cream cone in public looks 'childish' to most Japanese.

If you do step on Japanese toes (and this is sometimes unavoidable), at least try to convey the sincere impression that you are sorry. If stuck for Japanese words, using English is better than saying nothing at all, together with the appropriate gestures. Remember to apologize often, even for seemingly trivial mistakes. *Sumimasen* expresses general regret.

When making verbal decisions, especially over the phone, there is always the chance of being misunderstood. You may have trouble with the Japanised version of English words. One reason is the rule in Japanese that a consonant is followed by a vowel (rather like Italian). This can turn 'taxi' into *takushi*, etc. Conversely, rapidly-spoken 'English' —English can be misunderstood because American pronunciation is more widely used in Japan.

Always speak clearly and relatively slowly, but not insultingly so. Although most Japanese can read and correspond in English, they have little occasion to speak it. Therefore, avoid dialect, slang words, or puns. Don't raise your voice when misunderstood—either repeat your words slowly, or write them down if they are of importance.

Because of the value given to politeness, Japanese don't like you and others to realize that they frequently don't understand what you say. Even so, keep in mind that their understanding of your culture and language is likely to be much greater than yours is of theirs.

Don't be put off if long pauses occur in a conversation. To most Japanese, using English for any length of time is very tiring. The overall response time to a question may also be longer. Silences in conversation produce less anxiety than in the West. Avoid repeating your question with a raised voice, and try to listen more than usual.

Don't defend your viewpoint vehemently, thereby putting your partner in the wrong. Japanese will tend to agree with others just for the sake of preserving harmony—what they really think is another matter. In Japan this is not hypocrisy, but good manners.

There is a large amount of implicit trust in Japan, especially if you have had an introduction to some group. Questions are usually phrased in such a way that you can give an affirmative answer. Except for vital business decisions, you can often agree to something without having understood the question fully, and then hope for the best. Getting back to a child-like state of trust could be one of the many pleasant experiences of visiting Japan.

7

USEFUL PHRASES

Written Japanese is difficult; but elementary spoken Japanese can be acquired easily as will be seen in the sister volume to this book *Very Simple Japanese*. However, you will create a good impression if you make the effort to learn just a few phrases and words. The following are amongst those frequently required by the visitor:-

Mr/Mrs/Miss	. . . san *after* the surname (but don't ever append it to your own name).
Good morning	ohayō gozaimas'
Good day	kon-nichi wa
Good evening	konban wa
Good bye	Sayōnara
Good night (on retiring)	O-yasumi nasai
Hot, isn't it!	atsui des' nê!
Cold, isn't it!	samui des' nê!
Yes, I am listening	hai, hai
Yes, I agree	hai, sō des'
No (rarely used)	iie
No, I disagree	chigaimas'
Please (help yourself etc)	dōzo
Please give me . . .	. . . okudasai
On starting a meal	itadakimas'
Cheers!	kampai!
Thank you (for kindness)	dōmo arigatō gozaimash'ta
Thank you (after a meal)	gochisō-sama desh'ta
Thanks (for recent kindness shown)	kono aida wa dōmo arigatō gozaimash'ta

No thank you (I have had enough)	mō kekko des'
Excuse me (or: I am sorry)	sumimasen
It's all right	daijōbu des'
My name is . . .	. . . des' (*after* your surname)
Pleased to meet you	dōzo yoroshiku
You're welcome	dō itashimash'te
No, thank YOU	iie kochira koso
Pleased to meet you	hajimemash'te, ome ni kakarimas'
Where is . . .?	. . . wa doko des'ka
Please give me . . .	. . . o kudasai
How much does it cost?	. . . wa ikura des'ka?
I don't understand	wakarimasen
Who speaks English?	dare ka eigo o hanashimas'ka?
I don't understand Japanese	Nihongo ga wakarimasen
Please call a taxi	takushi o yonde kudasai
I want to go . . .	. . . ni ikitai des' ga
This is the address	kore wa jūsho des'
To the right	migi
To the left	hidari
Straight ahead	massugu
Stop	tomatte
Here	koko
There	asoko
Faster	motto hayaku
More slowly	motto yukkuri

Pronunciation:

Vowels similar to Italian or German:
a as in far
e as in men
i as in meet
o as in gone
u as in put

Consonant as in English, except:
g as in 'give' at the start of a word, otherwise ng as in 'sing'
s always hard, as in 'see'.

Vowels written here with a macron (−) should be lengthened. Words featuring an apostrophe (des'): the apostrophe replaces the vowel 'u' or 'i' which is not pronounced.